Emergency Vehicles
Police Car

Chris Oxlade

QED

QED Publishing

First published in the UK in 2009 by
QED Publishing
A Quarto Group company
226 City Road
London EC1V 2TT

www.qed-publishing.co.uk

A catalogue record for this book is available from the British Library.

ISBN 978 1 84835 268 1

Printed and bound in China

Author Chris Oxlade
Project Editor Eve Marleau
Designer Susi Martin

Publisher Steve Evans
Creative Director Zeta Davies
Managing Editor Amanda Askew

Picture credits
(t=top, b=bottom, l=left, r=right, c=centre, fc=front cover)
Alamy
4l Goss images; 6–7 Paul Springett A; 7r Justin Kase zfourz; 8–9 Howard Sayer; 10 ACE STOCK LIMITED; 11 Jack Sullivan; 12–13 fine art
Chris Taylor, with thanks to the Metropolitan Police
16–17, 17l
Corbis
9r DiMaggio/Kalish
Photolibrary
13r Thomas Frey
Shutterstock
1; 4–5 MalibuBooks; 14–15 Samuel Acosta; 15 Andresr; 18–19 Denise Kappa; 19r michael rubin; 21r Nicholas Rjabow; 20l Jenny Woodworth
www.ukemergency.co.uk
20–21

Words in **bold** can be found in the glossary on page 23.

Contents

What is a police car?

A police car is an **emergency** vehicle driven by police officers. They use police cars to control **traffic**, **patrol** the streets and chase criminals.

Not all police cars are big and fast. This is an electric city patrol car.

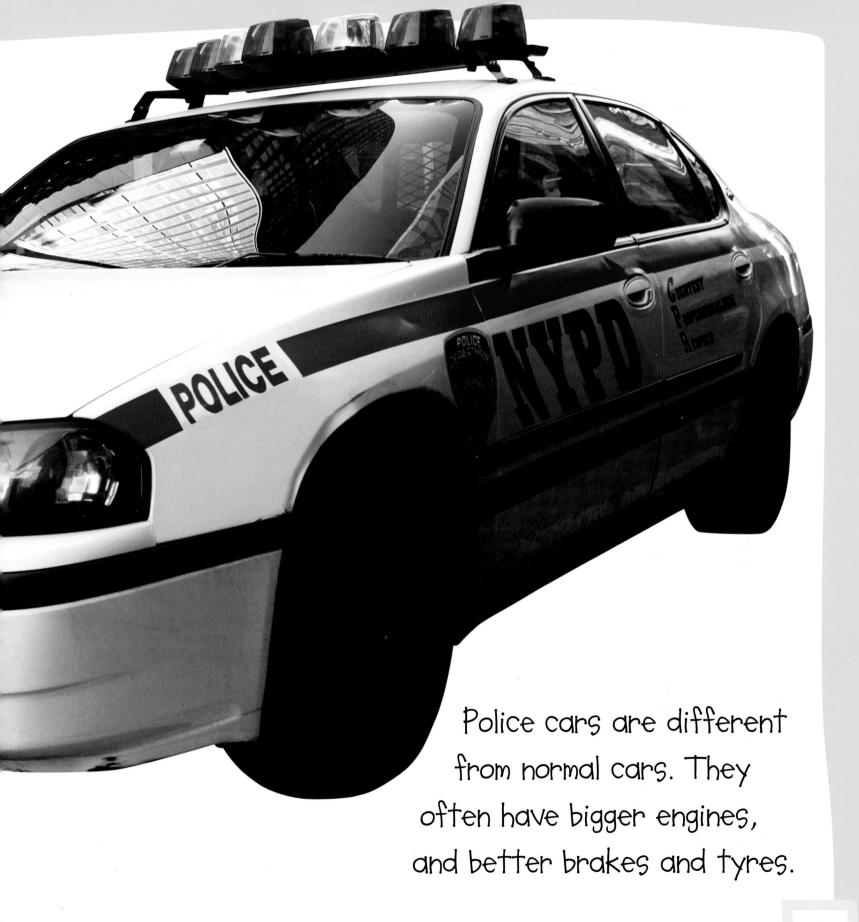

Police cars are different
from normal cars. They
often have bigger engines,
and better brakes and tyres.

Lights and sirens

Police cars have flashing lights and noisy **sirens**. Red-and-blue flashing lights warn other drivers that a police car is coming. Loud sirens make long screeching noises or blips.

Police cars have colourful blocks and stripes, so they can easily be seen.

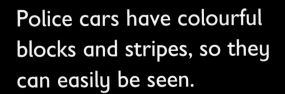

Some of the markings on police cars are **reflective**, which makes them shine at night. The markings make the cars easy for people to recognize.

A police officer uses lights and sirens to make sure people can see and hear the car.

Police car equipment

Police cars have lots of special equipment inside, including a **two-way radio**. Police officers use the radio to talk to other officers or the police headquarters.

These police officers are using their two-way radio to report an **incident**.

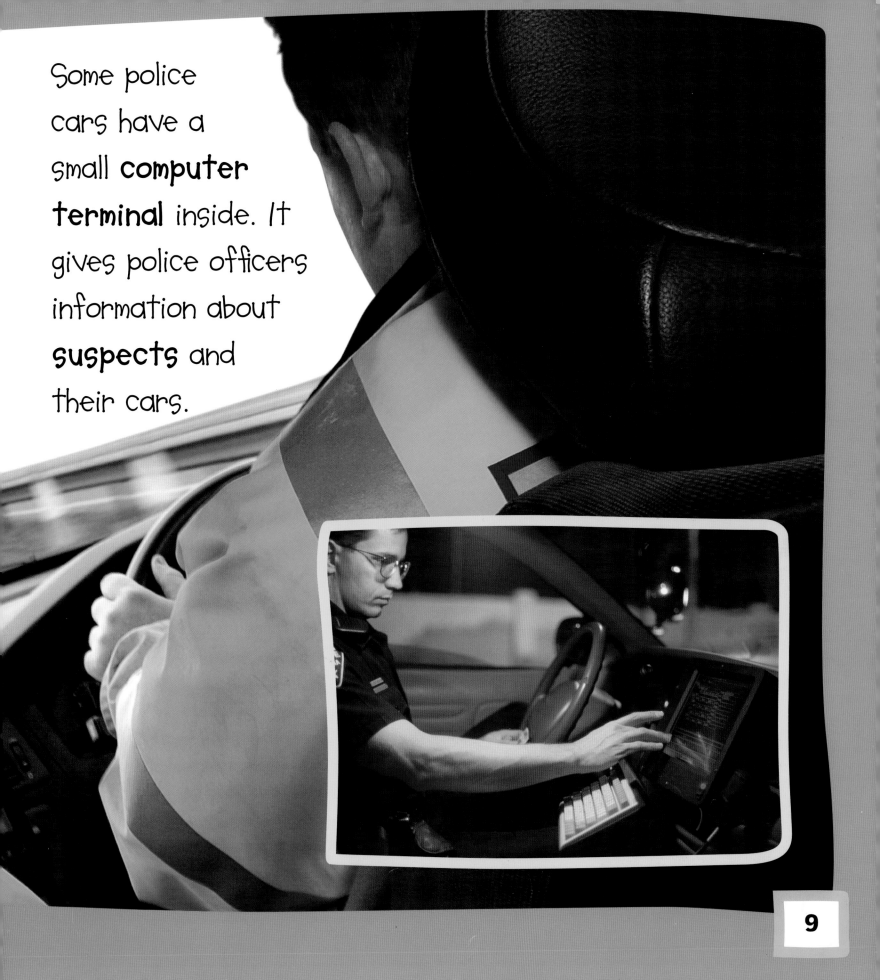

Some police cars have a small **computer terminal** inside. It gives police officers information about **suspects** and their cars.

High-speed cars

A pursuit car is a very fast police car. Police officers use them to chase criminals. Pursuit cars are normally powerful sports cars.

This Italian pursuit car is a Maserati sports car.

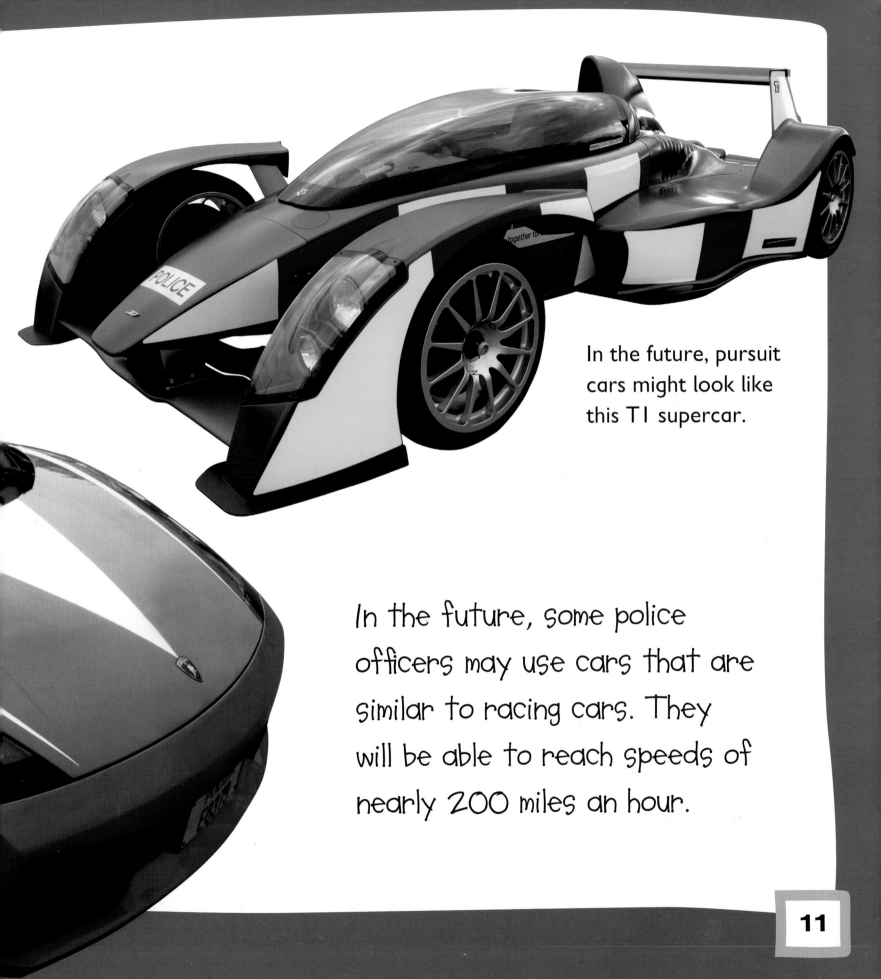

In the future, pursuit cars might look like this T1 supercar.

In the future, some police officers may use cars that are similar to racing cars. They will be able to reach speeds of nearly 200 miles an hour.

Special police cars

Police forces also have special-purpose cars. Some forces have rescue cars with **four-wheel drive** for going **off road**. They can be used to reach people on ground, such as sand, that normal cars cannot easily drive on.

EMERGENCY
CALL **911** FIRE POLICE MEDICAL

Other special police vehicles include mobile police command centres or armoured trucks for controlling large crowds.

This four-wheel drive police car is used on the beaches in California, USA.

Police vans

Police forces have vans for transporting people and equipment. Some police forces have teams of officers that deal with dangerous criminals who carry weapons. They travel in armoured vans.

This police van has a windscreen protector.

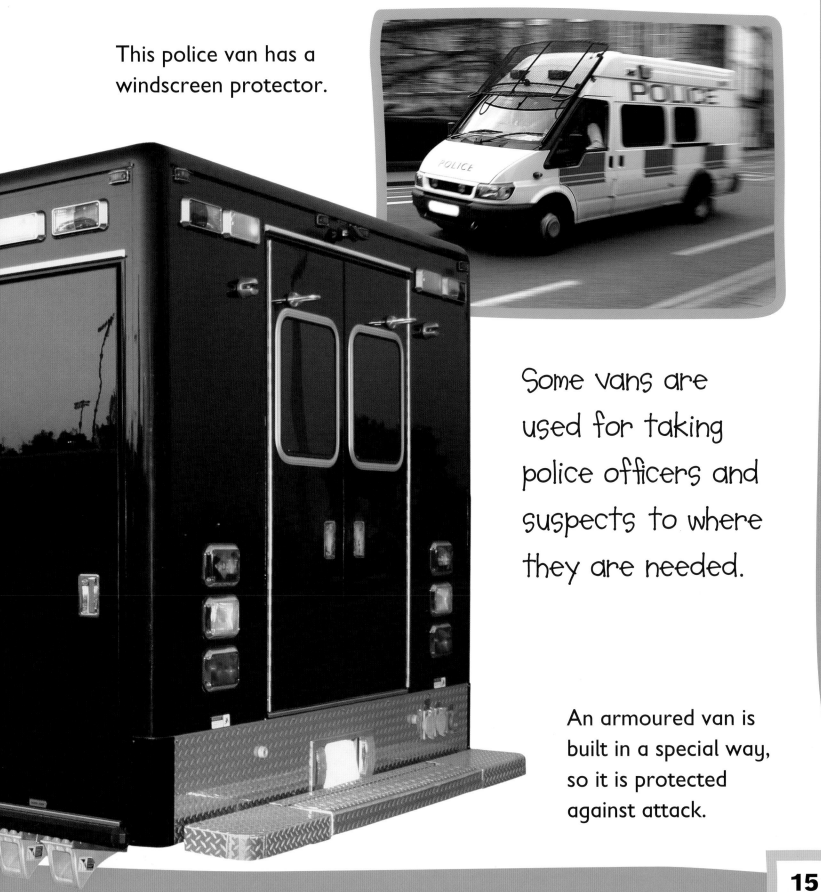

Some vans are used for taking police officers and suspects to where they are needed.

An armoured van is built in a special way, so it is protected against attack.

Driving a police car

Police officers have to drive fast when they are chasing suspects. This can be dangerous for the police officers and other drivers on the road, so they are specially trained to drive at high speeds.

Police officers must be able to control a car in any type of weather.

Police officers go to special driving schools. They learn the skills they need to drive safely at high speed, to stop quickly, and to control the car if they skid.

Police officers practise driving with two wheels off the road.

Police on two wheels

Police officers use motorcycles as well as cars. Motorcycles are good for moving through traffic in busy city streets. Traffic officers use them for patrolling motorways and for riding alongside cars transporting important people.

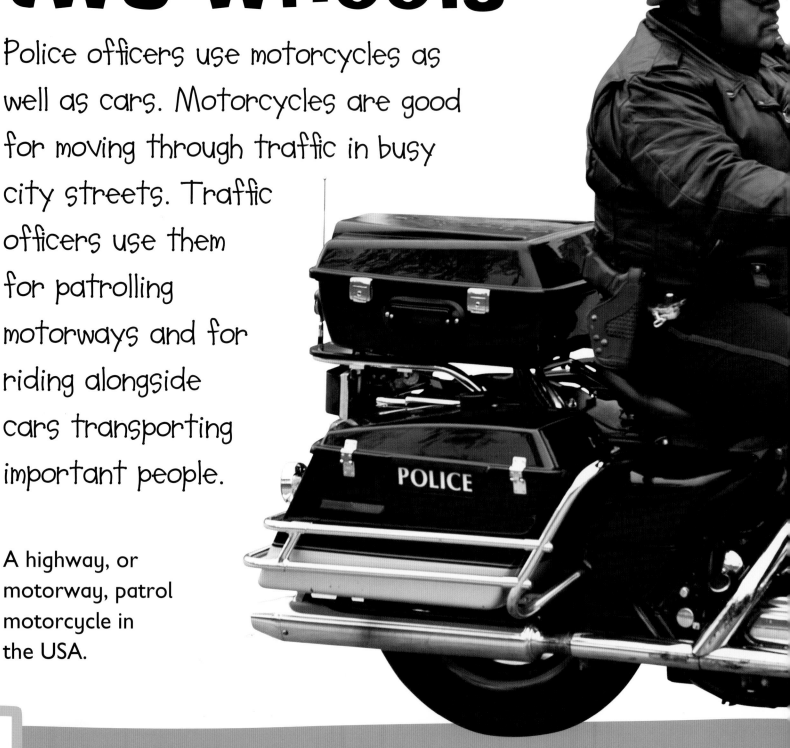

A highway, or motorway, patrol motorcycle in the USA.

Town and city
police officers
can travel more
quickly by bicycle
than on foot.

Land, air and sea

The police also use aircraft, horses and boats. Police use helicopters to follow criminals on the ground and to check for traffic jams. Police officers ride horses to patrol the streets.

Police officers are often seen on horseback in towns and cities.

Police use motorboats to patrol rivers and shorelines in cities. They can search suspicious boats and rescue people from the water.

Activities

- Which picture shows a police motorcycle, a pursuit car and a police boat?

- Make a drawing of your favourite police car. What sort of car is it? Does it have lights and sirens? What colour is it?

- Write a story about a police chase. It could be anywhere in the world – or even on another planet! What car would you drive? What crime would you be fighting? How dangerous would it be? How long would it take?

- Which of these police cars would be used to control a large crowd?

Glossary

Computer terminal
A machine that lets people look at information stored on a computer.

Emergency
A dangerous situation that must be dealt with straight away.

Four-wheel drive
Where all the wheels of a vehicle are turned by the engine.

Incident
Something that happens.

Off road
When a vehicle can be used on rough ground.

Patrol
To walk or drive around an area several times to check for trouble or danger.

Reflective
A material that light bounces off very well.

Siren
A machine that makes a loud, screeching noise.

Suspect
Someone who the police think is guilty of committing a crime.

Traffic
Cars, trucks, motorcycles and other vehicles on the road.

Two-way radio
A radio set that lets people talk to each other.

Index